eBay Selling Mastery 2016

How To Turn Your eBay Hobby To A Profitable SIX FIGURE Business

By Zack B.

Introduction

I want to thank you and congratulate you for downloading the book, *"ebay selling mastery 2016"*.

This book contains my proven steps and strategies on how to succeed as en ebay seller.

At the beginning of my journey (2008), I sold pretty much EVERYTHING I had laying around the house, made a few hundred dollars, but then ran into a very common problem that you are probably facing right now, as well of thousands of other ebay sellers : **I ran of out products to sell.**

Unlike other basic "eBay guides" out there, I won't focus on the technical side of ebay like how to register and eBay account or how to list an item, I'm sure you know how to do that (and if you don't google it, there's plenty of free info on the tech side of ebay).

Instead, I want to focus on what matters most in order to succeed.

If you want to turn your ebay business into a lean mean selling machine, you need to focus on two things:

1. Finding products that are in demand in the ebay marketplace
2. Finding sources where you can get these products at cheap prices

These are the two things I focused on when writing this ebook.

After years of trial and error, I finally figured out how to turn my eBay hobby into a 6 figure business (in June,2016, my sales on ebay grossed $35,941) and I decided to write this book in order to help you achieve similar success on your business.

Thanks again for downloading this book, I'm sure you will find a lot of value in it.

© Copyright 2016 by Zack B. - All rights reserved.

This document is geared towards providing exact and reliable information in regards to the topic and issue covered. The publication is sold with the idea that the publisher is not required to render accounting, officially permitted, or otherwise, qualified services. If advice is necessary, legal or professional, a practiced individual in the profession should be ordered.

- From a Declaration of Principles which was accepted and approved equally by a Committee of the American Bar Association and a Committee of Publishers and Associations.

In no way is it legal to reproduce, duplicate, or transmit any part of this document in either electronic means or in printed format. Recording of this publication is strictly prohibited and any storage of this document is not allowed unless with written permission from the publisher. All rights reserved.

The information provided herein is stated to be truthful and consistent, in that any liability, in terms of inattention or otherwise, by any usage or abuse of any policies, processes, or directions contained within is the solitary and utter responsibility of the recipient reader. Under no circumstances will any legal responsibility or blame be held against the publisher for any reparation, damages, or monetary loss due to the information herein, either directly or indirectly.

Respective authors own all copyrights not held by the publisher.

The information herein is offered for informational purposes solely, and is universal as so. The presentation of the information is without contract or any type of guarantee assurance.

The trademarks that are used are without any consent, and the publication of the trademark is without permission or backing by the trademark owner. All trademarks and brands within this book are for clarifying purposes only and are the owned by the owners themselves, not affiliated with this document.

Table Of Contents

Introduction 3
Chapter 1 : eBay Facts and Figures - The $82 Billion Monster 6
Chapter 2 : Product Research Made Easy – Finding A Profitable Product That SELLS ! 7
Chapter 3 : Buying Single Items & Flipping Them For Profits (Retail Arbitrage) 12
Chapter 4: Buying Bulk - Wholesalers, Liquidation Pallets & More 15
Chapter 5 : Better Listings, More Sales 19
Chapter 6 : Turning Your eBay Hobby To a Business in 4 Simple Steps 23
Conclusion 28

Chapter 1 : eBay Facts and Figures - The $82 Billion Monster

In 2015 alone, eBay enabled a mind-boggling $82,000,000,000 (that's billion dollars, with a B!) of gross merchandise volume.

That means over $82 Billion worth of products were sold on eBay in 2015! That's INSANE.

In 2016s' second quarter alone(!!!), eBay reported a whooping gross merchandise volume of **$20.9B**.

Founded in 1995 in San Jose, CA, eBay is one of the biggest, most lucrative online marketplaces.

One of eBays' biggest advantages is having the perception of the cheapest prices online in consumers' eyes, which is not always true, but definitely gives us sellers a HUGE advantage.

Online sales are going up each year and I, like many other, predict the same in the future. While retail stores go down in sales, online stores are KILLING IT !

If you need further evidence that in todays' world everyone buy stuff online, ask 5 of your friends if they have bought something online in the past 3 months. I guarantee you that at least 4 of them will say they did.

Whether you want to make some extra income to pay your bills or create a 6 figure business, I highly encourage you to start your own eBay business, and start it NOW.

Chapter 2 : Product Research Made Easy – Finding A Profitable Product That SELLS !

One of my favorite sayings is "<u>success love preparation</u>". It's just so true.

If you go ahead and buy a ton of product without knowing if they sell well, you will waste money, time, energy, and the worst thing is you can get discouraged quickly.

First, you need to choose a niche / industry you will stick to when selling on ebay.

You can buy random items and resell them, but from my experience, sticking to an industry is not just more profitable, it makes it easier.

For instance, I sell a lot of HBA items (health and beauty aids) in one of my accounts, in fact I stick to HBA items only in this particular account.

I have regular costumers that come back regularly for new products. They know my store sells HBA and I get new supplies every month, so it became their "go-to" place when they want to buy these items.

They will never go to my ebay store and suddenly find car parts or t-shirts, because I make sure to customize each account and stick to 1 industry in it.

If you're having a hard time choosing a niche (like most people who start on ebay) you're not alone. There are just so many options out there.

For start, I suggest you write down your all of your hobbies (surfing, singing, and so on) and then write down all the products that are related to each hobby.

So using our example of surfing, the item list can be :

- Wetsuits
- Surfboards
- Sun screen
- Swim suits
- Surfboard covers
- Beach Bags

And so on...

I love this exercise and use it a lot, you can find awesome products and niches with it.

Lets say you don't have any hobbies, what should you do then ?

Just go to **ebay** and look at the different **categories**.

Then, make a list of products from each category.

After you have a list of items you could sell, you need to find out 2 things :

1. Are **these items in high demand on ebay** ? (I'll talk more about researching demand next)
2. Can you find **a reliable source** (wholesaler, liquidation source, or any other source) that can supply you the products, in a **cheap price** that will leave room for a **profit when you resell it** ?

Lets say I chose "wetsuits" from our example earlier.

Next, I need to check the demand for wetsuits on ebay, find a wholesaler or a source where I can buy them from, and I'm ready to start my wetsuit store.

When it comes to profitability, ask yourself :

1. What is the price it is LIKELY to sell for ?
2. What is the price I will pay for it ?
3. What will be the net profit (after shipping & fees) you will make when the item is sold ?

That is exactly the process I use in order to determine whether a product is worth going for.

Checking the demand for an item on ebay is pretty simple.

First, type the product name in the search box on eBay, and tick the " sold listings " option on the left.

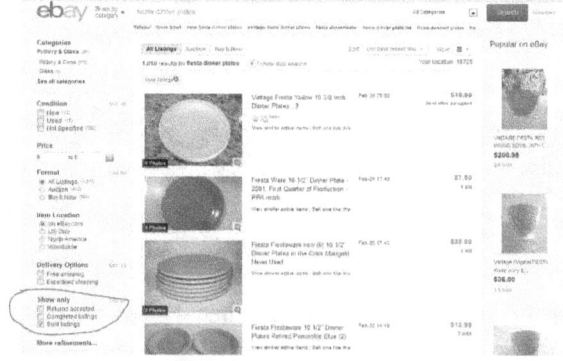

The "sold listings" feature on ebay.

Then, look at the prices and dates of the items sold.

Ask yourself these questions :

1. Did your item sell frequently, or does it sell a couple here and there ?
2. Does the average price it sold for, meets your expectation?
3. Is there one seller that sells the most and basically dominates the industry? (if there is, it should be a warning sign, can you get better pricing than this guy? How are you going to compete with him?)

From my experience when buying products to resell on eBay, many times the price you think it will sell for, DOESN'T MATCH the price it actually sales for.

Make sure you have the right data before you order products, it will save you a ton of time, money and energy.

The 'sold listings' will give you a very strong indication on the amount of products you could sell.

Obviously there are tweaks that you can and must do in order to sell more but if the item doesn't sell well to begin with, look for the next item.

Live to fight another day.

Another great indication for the demand of an item, **is** **http://WatchCount.com.**

WatchCount is one of my favorite eBay tools, and its FREE!

It shows you an estimate of how many of this item were sold, **and** how many people "watch" this item, **and** what price it sales for. **Now that is some awesome data, isn't it?**

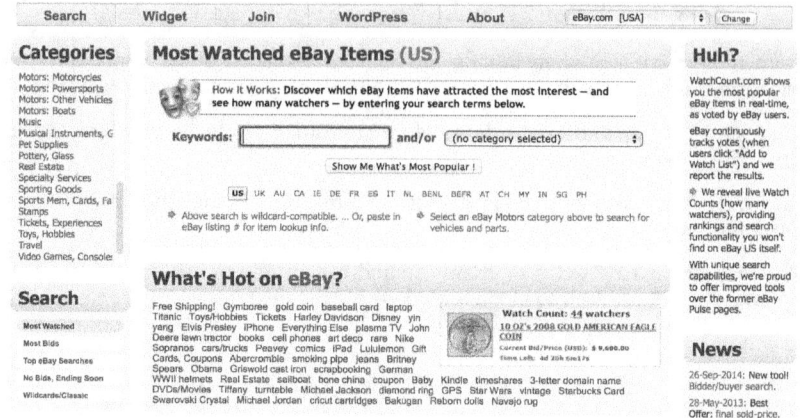

WatchCount.com is one of the most powerful eBay tools, use it !

After you figured out the demand for the item, you need to find a source.

In chapters three and four I talk more about suppliers, including wholesalers, liquidation supplies and more.

After you find out the price you get from the source, make sure to calculate the NET PROFIT.

This is where a lot of eBay sellers get confused and miss important points.

When calculating the net profit of an item, here's what you need to consider:

1. Your cost per item
2. Shipping fees (I highly recommend using the free shipping option unless it's a big, heavy item)
3. Ebay & PayPal fees (around 15% of the sold price)

If you got a little confuse, don't worry, I got the solution for you !

Go to http://finalfeecalculator.com - it's another powerful, free tool that will show you exactly what's your net profit !

When it comes to the "recommended net profit " that's up to you. Obviously you want to make the most money out of each sale. I recommend to sticking with items in the $20-80 range if you're just starting out.

When selling high ticket items, you will need more money to start with and are playing a riskier game, that can be profitable but you better know what you're doing.

With that being said, I don't recommend selling low ticket.

Not only you will need to sell in high volumes in order to make some profit, most of these " cheap " items are also sold by Chinese factories that can cut your price by half and outsell you every time.

If you still decide to sell cheap products and want to beat the Chinese factories, here's a tip : **emphasis the fact that you're a US seller and ship extremely fast.**

People are willing to pay more in order to get their item within 2 days Vs. 3 weeks from China. There's your competitive edge!

Now that we know how to analysis the demand for the item and the profitability, lets talk about where you can buy products from !

Chapter 3 : Buying Single Items & Flipping Them For Profits (Retail Arbitrage)

So you have found an eBay item / niche you would like to sell products in, and now need to find these products in competitive price in order to make a profit on.

When I started my eBay business, this was my biggest challenge. I simply couldn't find good product sources. **Luckily for you, you won't be dealing with this problem because of this book.**

In this chapter, I listed all of the product sources I currently use. Feel free to use the right one for you, and remember, if you're buying from wholesalers, more often than not, you will need to start your own LLC (many of them will ask for resell license).

I will cover 2 ways you can buy supply in :

1. Buying single items (individual purchases)
2. Buy in bulk (big quantities of the same or different items)

When buying single items in order to resell for a profit (often refered to as "retail arbitrage") you will usually not get wholesale prices. For instance, you will buy a rolex watch from some lady that purchased it and need the money, so she will sell it with a 50% loss on her side. You can then sell the rolex on ebay for a higher price **because you bought it for a lower price than it's market value.**

Where can you find products that sell for a cheap price ? start locally!

Using Your Local Market To Your Advantage -

One of the best ways to buy products for resell purposes is your local market, because you will have less competition. I can't buy items from your local area if I live in Miami, Florida and you're in Pheonix, Arizona.

Another great thing about buying locally (from other people in your area or local stores) is **that you can find some real bargains for dirt cheap prices**, and are dealing with people who aren't necessarily thinking about making profits.

I made a ton of sales (and money) using that method. Just recently I bought a Movado watch from a guy in my area, for just $150, and later on sold it on eBay for $1000. That's about $700 [after fees] in net profit for that watch. Easy money baby!

Here are some great places to find products from your local area :

Thrift stores

Dollar stores

Retail stores that are going out of business (**huge opportunity**, recently Sports Authority were going out of business in Florida, it made me over 10,000 in net profit)

Small "mom&pops" & local shops

Craigslist.com

Garage sells

Local Flea Markets (you can find real gems on flea markets, believe me)

If you like using apps, there are some that I regularly use to find bargains.

Apps you can use to find local sellers :

Offer up (my favorite)

Letgo

Varagesale

Buying from local people is always a good idea. You can negotiate and often meet people who are very eager to get rid of their item and will sell it for dirt cheap!

Keep in mind you can also buy single products online and resell them on eBay for a profit. Heck, you can even buy items on eBay then resell them on eBay!

You just have to be creative, and know your market. I love watches and sell many of them, I know exactly what a watch will sell for. That's power.

Here's a quick story of how **I made around $500** with the 'best offer' option on ebay with just **a few clicks** : A couple days ago I was browsing on eBay and saw a Tag Heuer (a luxury watch brand) that is worth around **$1200**, and it was selling for $850.

Awesome, I could make a couple hundred dollars of profit just by buying and reselling it on ebay right? That's true, but instead of using the "buy now" option, I used the **"best offer"** option, and got the watch for **$500.**

Now that's a nice profit, in a matter of a few minutes. Be creative my friend !

Look for items that have the "best offer" option (you can sort it in the advanced search on ebay) and make sure to use it.

You can buy some real bargains that way, and the "best offer" should show you that the seller is willing to negotiate and obviously take a lower price, why else would he choose to give the best offer option ?

Buying on other websites and selling on eBay –

There are many deals on websites that will offer lower prices than eBay for some products.

You can always buy these and resell them, or you can "drop ship" (by posting the item on eBay and when the buyer buys, just ship it to his address from the other website)

Some of these deals sites I use are :

Groupon.com

FatWallet.com

Offer.com

Decide.com

FreeShippingDeals.org

Woot.com

I hope that gave you at least some ideas of where to look for bargains.

The list above is a great source and can make you a lot of money. It did for me.

You will have to be **persistent** and it is of course more time consuming than dealing with a wholesaler that will constantly ship you your products, but it is also very fun, at least for some of us.

Chapter 4: Buying Bulk - Wholesalers, Liquidation Pallets & More

It is hard to make a 6 figure eBay business with what I call "local hustle".

If you want to go bigger (and have the capital to invest), you will need to find a constant stream of a product that will make you constant profits.

There are 2 ways you can do just that:

1. Buy bulk random items for cheap prices per unit (liquidations, surplus supplies, out of business supplies and so on)
2. Find a wholesaler / manufacture that will supply a more specific product for a cheap, wholesale price.

I personally do both.

I love buying pallets of costumer returns for instance, and then reselling them on eBay.

Costumer return products, are basically products that were purchased and then returned to the store by the costumer.

You can buy pallets of different costumer returns, in different niches (I usually buy pallets of sports & outdoor gear).

But be careful: before you buy customer returns you MUST get the most information that you can.

I listed below websites that sell pallets of costumer returns, most of them will attach a **"manifest"(product list),** research it, see what the products are worth and always calculate your profit by the "worst case scenario " – some products you receive might be broken and you will have to take a loss.

You can resell them as bulk or separately, both are profitable in my experience, while if you sell each item separately, you will obviously make more money, and have to invest more time doing so.

Below are some of my favorite places to buy liquidated items.

Marketplaces for liquidation & surplus supplies:

Bulq.com

Bstock.com

GencoMarketPlace

Closeoutservices.com

Liquidation.com

Closeoutservices.com

AAA Online Auctions

Dollar Days

JD Closeouts

Liquidation Overstock

LiquidXS.com

Pallets Mart

Salvage Closeouts

Save On Closeouts

Via Trading Corporation

Wholesale Central

Wholesale University

D.J.H. Inc.

Wholesale Directory

1 ABC Closeouts

1 Liquidators Inc

1st Choice Surplus Merchandise

ABC Wholesale Products

All of the above are legit, and I used them before. I remember when I goggled some of them online I saw some good reviews and some bad reviews.

One review said " some of the products I got don't work ! "(duh!) obviously, the guy didn't know what he was doing.

With all the scammers online it became hard to find reliable sources, **so stick to the list above.**

Buying Products From Wholesalers / Factories –

If buying liquidated supplies doesn't seem appeal to you, you can always buy wholesale from suppliers / wholesalers / manufacturers.

As I said earlier, when buying from wholesalers more often than not, you will need to register an LLC and have the proper licenses, that's where you take your business a step further.

You can use LegalZoom to register an LLC, or you can use an accountant, it takes a few days and it's a pretty simple process, but its very necessary if you want to buy from wholesalers.

When looking for wholesalers, you need to get creative.

While there are some lists of wholesalers that I use (and will share with you) sometimes a 'Google search' is the best way to find what you seek.

Here are some search queries I google when looking for a wholesaler for a specific item :

" Item name + wholesaler "

"Item name + wholesale"

"Item name + bulk "

" Item name + surplus"

" Item name + Stock "

That actually landed me some great results and I have found some suppliers that weren't even listed in popular wholesaling websites.

You can also call a company and ask if they offer wholesale programs, you will be amazed on how many of them will do that, and even drop ship the product for you !

Be bold, take action, and be afraid to pick up the phone and cold call a company, you are doing them a favor too! These companies want to sell more, don't they?

With that being said, there are some great lists of verified wholesalers that I recommend you take a look at if you have a product in mind.

My List of wholesalers + Suppliers :

Wholesalers lists of USA suppliers -

Salehoo.com [my favorite]

Doba.com

LuxuryWholeSale

Wholesale Designer Handbags

WorldWideBrands.com

Wholesalers From Overseas (Mainly China) -

AliBaba.com

DhGate.com

AliExpress.com

When contacting wholesalers, keep in mind that you will sometime need to purchase bigger quantities than you initially planned.

Some wholesalers have MOQ (minimum order quantity) of 1 unit while others have an MOQ of 10,000 units, keep in mind that it can always be negotiated.

Chapter 5 : Better Listings, More Sales

Finding products in great prices is critical, but until they are sold, you won't make any money whatsoever.

In this chapter, I will share some of my most powerful tips on how to make sure your items actually sell, how to create powerful listings, and how to dominate your competition on eBay.

First, and probably the most important factor that will determine if your item will sell on eBay or will collect dust in your house (or warehouse) is your listing.

The 3 Elements of the Ultimate Listing :

1. The listings' title
2. Pictures of the product
3. Description of the product

It took me a while to decide whether the title should go first or product pictures, but I ended up choosing **the title of your listing to be the most critical because it is the #1 factor that ranks your item in eBays marketplace.**

What makes a good title for your listing?

When writing a listing title, you need to consider 2 things :

1. Keywords
2. Make it attractive so people want to click

First, make sure you write the name of the product.

For instance, if I'm selling a Movado watch that is black and model number 123,

I will start my title with "Movado Mens Watch Model 123 Black". The keywords should appear first. More often than not, I see listings on eBay that go like (with the Movado example): "BRAND NEW, COOL MOVADO WATCH, MINT "

That's a bad title. When writing the title and looking for the right keyword, simply type the name of your item into ebays search engine.

Then, the "auto-complete" will show you what people are typing when searching for this item. Use these keywords first.

So why do we need to make it attractive ?

First thing we need to do is make your listing come in the top results, and second, we need people to click it. That's why.

Add words like "NEW ! " , " STUNNING ! " , "BARGAIN ! " , "SALE! " at the end of your title, as long as it doesn't compromise some critical info about your item.

If you think, for instance, there is a more important detail you need to specify in the title vs adding the "click attracting words", do it.

A good title for the Movado watch will be : " Mens Black Movado Watch Model 123, NEW ! "

You always want to include specific information like model number, because this will drive you ultra-focused buyers that typed that exact model number, and therefore giving you a better chance that they will buy.

I've been doing SEO (search engine optimization) for years so it comes pretty easy for me, but I understand it can be confusing.

So when writing your title and choosing keywords, try to think what the buyer would type in the search box in order to find your item, vs. trying to describe the item in your own words. That will help you get the perfect "seo" title.

Product Pictures :

Another critical part of your listing in the pictures of the product you are selling.

When people ask me "how many pictures should I upload" I always reply '12'.

12 is the maximum pictures eBay allows you to upload for FREE(you can upload more but it will start costing you money, and in most cases its unnecessary).

I know you're human and probably don't always have the patience to upload 12 pictures every time, but on the other side, I don't care what product you're selling, you should NEVER EVER upload just 1 picture. Never. It doesn't make sense.

Even if you sell iPhones, products that pretty much every person on the planet is familiar with, you want to upload more pictures. Yes, even if its brand new in box.

Why?

Because people like pictures. And you want people to stay on your listing.

When you upload 3-6 pictures of that new in box iphone, it feels more informative. I'm not just guessing here, I have tested it myself and talked to other power sellers on eBay that confirmed the same thing.

When it comes to pictures : the more the better. Make sure you take pictures of every angle of your product, front, back, both sides, and so on...

When taking the pictures, make sure they are clear and avoid strong lighting or glares.

If you're selling small items or jewelry, I recommend holding the item, it gives it a more appealing look. If you're selling watches, like I do, more often than not, I will wear the watch myself and take a picture of my arm. In my experience, these kind of listings worked better.

Product Description :

When it comes to the description, I would suggest to keep it informative and SHORT. The fact is, people DON'T like to read. That's why you should give every piece of information possible in the title, without it looking too messy, of course.

Think about it, when was the last time you went on eBay and read the WHOLE description?

Probably never, unless it was a few sentences short.

Keep your listings informative, but at the same time, short and to the point.

Here's my recommended format of an item description :

Item Name (just copy the title here)

Item Description:

Feature 1

Feature 2

Feature 3

Shipping & Handling Policy

Return Policy

That's pretty much it. Of course this is a very general format but im trying to give you an idea.

Always have a shipping & handling policy, and always have a return policy. Even if you choose to not accept returns, state it. (although its not smart, because in most cases eBay will make you accept the return anyway).

To sum things up, make sure your listings are always informative and appealing. Make sure the pictures are clear, if the item is defected, always state it.

Don't forget to include size, color and technical details of the item.

When creating the listing remember that most people are lazy and won't read your whole listing, that's why the pictures and title should give a good idea of what you're selling.

Chapter 6 : Turning Your eBay Hobby To a Business in 4 Simple Steps

If you want to turn your ebay "hobby" to a business, and by that I mean scaling up, and sell (a lot) more on ebay, the first thing you need to change is your mindset.

Treat it like a business, not a hobby

The entry barrier is pretty low (and cheap) when it comes to online entrepreneurship in general (lets call it making money online...) MOST people I know are **not treating it seriously enough**.

I write a blog that makes me an additional income for instance, and I had a friend asking me what he should do in his blog in order to achieve the same success I did.

See, he started a blog, wrote some good content, but nothing happened since.

He writes a post "when he feels like it" like he says, and that's not the way businesses work. **He treats it like a hobby.**

The same exact mindset exists in many ebay sellers minds. They register an account, list a few items, some sell, some don't....

Imagine owning a physical business, lets say you're in the car wash industry.

If you started a physical business like that, wouldn't you have a **solid game plan**?

Wouldn't you have **goals** to reach **every month**?

wouldn't you have to **TAKE MASSIVE ACTION marketing** your car wash business ?

You will need to advertise your business, online, offline, maybe even cold call prospects, and for sure you would have told your friends & family to come to your new business and check it out, wouldn't you?

Then my question is, **why don't you treat your eBay business the same way you would a physical business ?**

I treat my ebay business like any regular business. I have a business plan for it, I have a marketing plan I wrote, I have goals that I need to reach every month, of course I registered an LLC for it, I have an accountant that is in charge of taxes.

It's a business ! treat it like one !

Step 1 : Set up goals

One of my favorite quotes ever, by Lewis Carrol, is :

"Alice: Would you tell me, please, which way I ought to go from here?

The Cheshire Cat: That depends a good deal on where you want to get to.

Alice: I don't much care where.
The Cheshire Cat: Then it doesn't much matter which way you go.
Alice: ...So long as I get somewhere.
The Cheshire Cat: Oh, you're sure to do that, if only you walk long enough."

The bottom line is, you MUST set goals, in your ebay business as well as in everything in your life.

If you won't have a goal, how do you know if you're winning ? If you can't measure it, you won't be able to improve!

Set up a goal to your ebay business. How much do you want to sell each month ? $1,000 ? $2,000? $20,000 ?

Once I wrote my eBay goals down it changed everything for me.

Because I then did the math, and I could see exactly how to get there ! (which is the next step we'll talk about).

Step 2 : Write a game plan

Now that you have a goal, you know what you where you want to go and how much your ebay business need to make every month, write a game plan that will have practical steps that will get you to your goals.

Do the math, it's so simple.

For instance, lets say you want to sell $10,000 worth of goods every month.

Your products average net profit is $20.

How many products do you need to sell per day in order to reach your goal ?

In our example, the number is around 17 sales per day.

And now you know that all you need to do in order to make $10,000 per month from your ebay business, is to sell 17 products each day.

So how do you sell 17 products a day?

What actions do you need to take ?

How much marketing do you need to do in order to sell 17 items a day ?

See, that's the reason I love writing game plans. After we calculate everything, it looks much easier to reach our goal, doesn't it ?

The problem is most people don't do the math.

It doesn't need to be a technical one with business terms. Just write your plan in your own words.

Answer these questions in your business plan :

- What kind of products will I focus on ? what's my niche ?
- Where do I buy these items ?
- How will I attract buyers to my store ?
- How often will I ship items to buyers ?
- What is my return policy ?
- What is my shipping & handling policy ?

Step 3 : TAKE MASSIVE ACTION !

Remember the old saying " knowledge is power "? Well, that's not entirely true in our case.

Knowledge without action will take you nowhere. You have to put in the work.

After you have created a plan, you know your goals and targets; you must put in some work.

I start every morning looking for new products and ideas that can make me more money.

That's the first thing I do every day, I have been doing it since 2009. Focus on what makes you money. Always be on the hunt for good deals & products.

Look for trends (use Google trends to see what's trending), recently when the "Pokémon go" game was released, I quickly bought Pokémon go shirts from a friend, that made me around $8,000 so far, and counting...

Every new trend is an opportunity for you as an ebay seller. I disagree with those who say " stick to non-seasonal products that you can sell all year round". That's just dumb.

Obviously you want to sell these products all year long, but when Christmas comes, why not bank on that too?

At the time I'm writing this book, we're pretty close to August, "back to school" times. Why wouldn't you want to use that in your advantage? I know I am. I brought in a shipment of back packs for kids (using <u>Salehoo.com</u>) I won't be selling these after the "back to school" period ends, but right now they sell like hell, so why not ?

It doesn't interfere with my other products as I have several ebay accounts(which I suggest you do too), and one of them is used for seasonal products.

I recommend you consider outsourcing the tasks you don't like about eBay and focus on making money. Consider using a fulfillment center (google it) that will ship the products for you.

I hate listing items, I think its boring, so I hired a VA (virtual assistance) that does that for me.

It doesn't make sense for me to list my own items, because its time consuming and it's a task that my VA can do even better than me after I explained to her what I wanted (thanks Jessica).

That way I get to do the stuff that are more important, like finding opportunities and deals, and expanding my business.

You can find hire people that will gladly help you with your business on odesk.com or elance.com.

I attended a lecture of a multi millionaire who said " I don't wash my own dishes not because I'm lazy, just because I use my time to create more money. It just doesn't make sense to do the dishes or other tasks around the house while I can make a hundred thousand on a deal instead".

I love that way of thinking.

Focus on **what matters most in your business,** outsource the rest.

Step 4 : Track Your Data, Analyze & Improve

Always track your data. Then at the end of every month, analyze it, see what you did right and where you can improve.

If some product didn't sell well, maybe you need to find a new product or improve the listing. Maybe you should list it as an auction, or maybe even sell it in bulk (try listing it as a pack...)

Maybe you can order another product that is related to it, and sell them as a set.

Track your data, track your sales, which item sold the most? Which items didn't? when did most of the sales occur ? did your items sell better on an auction vs. fixed price listings ? and so on...

Tracking, analyzing and improving the way you do thing is a crucial part of any business, especially one that wants to grow and improve.

Conclusion

Selling on eBay can be very profitable when done right, eventually it will all depend on your strategy and the amount of action you take.

I have some friends who make millions on eBay alone, and some are happy with just paying the rent & bills with their ebay income, both are perfectly fine and both will improve the way you live.

The biggest problem ebay sellers and other online entrepreneurs face is procrastination. They dwell on things that don't really matter or trying to be "perfect" and that leads to confusion and not taking any action at all.

Remember 'Pareto Rule' which says " 80% of the results will come from 20% of your actions " (read this line again to fully understand what it means).

Make sure you implement at least one idea from this book, even if you fail, at least you will learn what doesn't work for you and you can then focus on what works.

If you want to your eBay business to be extremely successful,

Thank you again for downloading this book! I really appreciate it.

I hope this book was able to help you and gave you some value, even 1 idea can change everything, believe me, I know.

If you have any suggestions for my book or questions in regards to your ebay business, email me at : Zionbar01@gmail.com , I'll be glad to help !

Finally, if you enjoyed this book, then I'd like to ask you for a favor, would you be kind enough to leave a review for this book on Amazon? It'd be greatly appreciated!

Click here to leave a review for this book on Amazon!

Thank you and good luck with your ebay business !

www.ingramcontent.com/pod-product-compliance
Lightning Source LLC
Chambersburg PA
CBHW070341190526
45169CB00005B/2001